Richard Alexander Fullerton Penrose

A Discourse Commemorative of the Life and Character of

Hugh L. Hodge

Richard Alexander Fullerton Penrose

A Discourse Commemorative of the Life and Character of Hugh L. Hodge

ISBN/EAN: 9783337817046

Printed in Europe, USA, Canada, Australia, Japan

Cover: Foto ©Thomas Meinert / pixelio.de

More available books at **www.hansebooks.com**

COMMEMORATIVE OF THE LIFE AND CHARACTER

OF

HUGH L. HODGE, M.D., LL.D.,

LATE EMERITUS PROFESSOR OF OBSTETRICS AND DISEASES
OF WOMEN AND CHILDREN

IN THE

UNIVERSITY OF PENNSYLVANIA.

BY

R. A. F. PENROSE, M.D.,

PROFESSOR OF OBSTETRICS AND DISEASES OF WOMEN AND CHILDREN.

DELIVERED OCTOBER 6th, 1873,

BEFORE THE

TRUSTEES, PROFESSORS, AND STUDENTS OF THE UNIVERSITY OF PENNSYLVANIA.

PHILADELPHIA:
COLLINS, PRINTER, 705 JAYNE STREET.
1873.

A DISCOURSE

COMMEMORATIVE OF THE LIFE AND CHARACTER

OF

HUGH L. HODGE, M.D., LL.D.,

LATE EMERITUS PROFESSOR OF OBSTETRICS AND DISEASES
OF WOMEN AND CHILDREN

IN THE

UNIVERSITY OF PENNSYLVANIA.

BY

R. A. F. PENROSE, M.D.,

PROFESSOR OF OBSTETRICS AND DISEASES OF WOMEN AND CHILDREN.

DELIVERED OCTOBER 6th, 1873,

BEFORE THE

TRUSTEES, PROFESSORS, AND STUDENTS OF THE UNIVERSITY OF PENNSYLVANIA.

PHILADELPHIA:
COLLINS, PRINTER, 705 JAYNE STREET.
1873.

CORRESPONDENCE.

At a meeting of the Medical Class of the University of Pennsylvania, held Oct. 10th, 1873, for the purpose of requesting a copy of Prof. Penrose's Introductory Lecture, Mr. John Ivison, of Philadelphia, was called to the Chair, and Mr. M. Frank Kirkbride, of Philadelphia, appointed Secretary.

On motion it was

Resolved, That a committee consisting of a representative from each State and country be appointed to carry out the intention of the Class.

UNIVERSITY OF PENNSYLVANIA,
Philadelphia, Oct. 13th, 1873.

DEAR SIR: The undersigned, a special committee, to whom the duty has been delegated of requesting for publication, a copy of your able and eloquent eulogy upon the life and character of our late lamented Professor, Hugh L Hodge, while communicating the wish of the Class, desire at the same time to add our personal solicitation that you will accede to the request. A compliance with the wish expressed through us will be not only a manifestation of your kindness to us but a gratification to the relatives and friends of him whose merits have been commemorated by you.

With high esteem we remain
your obedient servants,
JAMES T. PRIESTLEY, Pennsylvania.
H. TURNER BASS, North Carolina.
DAN'L M. GUITERAS, Cuba.
GEO. L. EYSTER, Nebraska.
WM. McD. MASTIN, Alabama.

DR. PENROSE.

1331 SPRUCE STREET,
Philadelphia, Oct. 20th, 1873.

GENTLEMEN: The Introductory Address which the Class, through you, has requested for publication, was written not only to illustrate the works and virtues of our lamented professor, but also that the instructive and noble lessons they conveyed might not be lost to us. I place the Lecture, therefore, with much pleasure at your disposal. Accept for yourselves as well as for each member of the Class, my kindest wishes, and believe me

Your obedient servant,
R. A F. PENROSE.

To Messrs. JAS. T. PRIESTLEY, H. TURNER BASS, DAN'L M GUITERAS, GEO. L. EYSTER, WM. McD. MASTIN.

COMMITTEE ON PUBLICATION.

JAMES T PRIESTLEY, Pennsylvania.	GEO. HAYWARD COBURN, New Brunswick.
H. TURNER BASS, North Carolina.	ALBION D. WEEKS, Maine.
GRANVILLE E. DICKINSON, Maryland.	FRANK W. STEBALTS, Austria.
WM. McD. MASTIN, Alabama.	A. ELDRIDGE CARPENTER, New Jersey.
GUILHERME ELLIS, Brazil.	GEO. L. EYSTER, Nebraska.
DAN'L M. GUITERAS, Cuba.	CHAS E. McKELVEY, New York.
WM. GAMBLE, Connecticut.	JOHN H. MORRISON, Ohio.
THOS. H. COOPER, Delaware.	R. WILMOT DEAVER, Pennsylvania.
CHAS. E. MATTESON, Illinois.	JOEL G. JUSTIN, Rhode Island.
THOS. W. MOORHEAD, Indiana.	ROBT. PILLOW, Tennessee.
AUSTIN L. FULLENWIDER, Iowa.	JOS H McDANIEL, Texas.
ALEX. M. STOUT, Kentucky.	CHAS. B. RUST, Jr, Virginia.
JAS. C. MERRILL, Massachusetts.	FRED. T. ABLE, Philadelphia.
V. GONZALES SALINAS, Mexico.	WM. BARTON HOPKINS, Philadelphia.
ABR. A. McDONALD, Minnesota.	LION REVORK GULISYAN, Turkey in Asia.
EDWIN D. FARROW, Missouri.	RICHARD J. METCALFE, Nova Scotia.

M. FRANK KIRKBRIDE,
Secretary.

JOHN IVISON,
Chairman.

Hugh L. Hodge, M.D., LL.D., Emeritus Professor of Obstetrics and Diseases of Women and Children in the University of Pennsylvania, died at his late residence, 901 Walnut Street, Philadelphia, on Wednesday morning, February 26th, 1873, at half past one o'clock.

His funeral took place from the Second Presbyterian Church, southeast corner of Twenty-first and Walnut Streets, on Saturday, March 1st, at one o'clock, the interment being at Laurel Hill.

Special meetings of the various societies and associations with which he had been connected were held, and resolutions of condolence, sympathy, and eulogy were passed.

At a special meeting of the Medical Faculty of the University of Pennsylvania, held on February 28th, 1873, the following resolutions were adopted :—

Resolved, That the Faculty have heard with sincere sorrow of the death of one who stood in the relation either of preceptor or of colleague to all the members of this body, and that it is due to his memory to express their high appreciation of his character as a man, and of his distinction as a professor.

That the pure and elevated principles of Dr. Hodge were illustrated in a life devoted to the service of his fellow men, and to the promotion of all efforts to benefit and ennoble humanity, while his disinterested, gentle, and humane prosecution of his profession placed him as an example before his brethren, and endeared him to the community in which he dwelt, as well as to those who sought his counsel from abroad.

That his efficient services as a teacher of his art, placed him in the front rank of the eminent men who have shed lustre on the Medical Department of the University of Pennsylvania.

That, by his lectures and publications, he has contributed to the advancement and improvement of his special branch of medicine, and aided in the dissemination of sound doctrine in medical science, and although for many years retired from the more arduous duties of his profession, his influence has been deeply felt and cordially acknowledged.

That the Faculty, gratefully remembering the many manifestations of his personal kindness and interest, sincerely condole with the family of Dr. Hodge in their bereavement, and feel that consolation for the loss sustained by them and by ourselves is found in the belief of his eternal gain.

R. E. ROGERS, M.D.,
Dean of the Medical Faculty.

At a subsequent meeting of the Medical Faculty it was *Resolved*, that the Professor of Obstetrics and Diseases of Women and Children, Dr. Penrose, be requested to prepare an address on " The Life and Character of Dr. Hodge," to be given as the Introductory Lecture at the opening of the school in October next.

A DISCOURSE.

A YEAR ago, to-day, the Medical Class of the University of Pennsylvania assembled to listen to the Introductory lecture delivered by my colleague, Professor Carson, commemorative of the life and character of Dr. Samuel Jackson, our late professor of the Institutes of Medicine. There sat with us, at that time, Dr. Hugh L. Hodge, who, as professor, and professor emeritus, for more than a third of a century, had been a tower of strength to our school; who had been a pupil or a colleague of those great men whose names and works we prize as part of our richest inheritance; his name had become a household word throughout the land; his earnest devotion to his profession; his unselfish sacrificings to his patients; his strong faith, munificent liberality and beautiful life had gained for him the love and respect of all men. Alas! gentlemen, *his* place to-day is vacant. Our beloved professor is dead, and I have been appointed, by the medical faculty, to deliver this introductory lecture, commemorative of his life and character.

Dr. Hodge was born in Philadelphia, on June 27th, 1796, at his father's house in Water Street. At that day Philadelphia was comparatively a small place, numbering about 50,000 inhabitants, and Water Street, now occupied solely for commercial purposes, then was considered desirable for residences —indeed, the whole city was built along the Delaware River front, and farm-houses and farms were to be found east of Broad Street.

Dr. Hodge's grandfather was Andrew Hodge, who emigrated to this country in 1730, and became a successful merchant of Philadelphia. Andrew Hodge came of that Scotch-

Irish Presbyterian stock that contributed so large a portion of the early settlers of Pennsylvania, and which has given so many great and good men to our country. This Scotch-Irish Presbyterian stock is so peculiar, and its influence on the earlier development of this country so marked, that it deserves more than mere passing notice. When we consider "that moral and intellectual traits follow down a race from father to son, reappearing often in remote descendants exactly as peculiarities of feature or disease do," we can readily perceive the vast influence of hereditary antecedents. This race came from the Saxon population of the south of Scotland and the north of Ireland. In reflecting on its origin, it would seem as if Providence had subjected it, for generations, to stern treatment and severe discipline, in order that those traits of character, which are so strongly marked in the stock, might be developed to the full measure of vigor and strength necessary for the accomplishment of the great work for which it was designed.

Great races and great men do not come by accident. They are the results of antecedent conditions and circumstances reaching often back for centuries. To adopt a style of expression, which would have well pleased the subject of this notice, we may say that Providence does not, as a rule, appear to work by miracles, but by regular, fixed, well-established physical laws; and one of these physical laws, now universally recognized, is that so admirably and scientifically enunciated and illustrated by Mr. Darwin and Mr. Wallace, called usually the "Law of Natural Selection," or the "Law of the Survival of the Fittest;" that "wise and beneficent law by which the improvement and perfection of the human race alone can be secured; that law in consequence of which the best specimens of a species survive, and become the progenitors of generations more perfect than those preceding them, thus tending to propagate an ever-improving and perfecting type of humanity." I have said that this great principle controlling the development of our race, has been enunciated and illustrated by Mr. Darwin and Mr. Wallace, but the *law* is no discovery of theirs; it was first proclaimed by the inspired pen of the great Jewish lawgiver, who frequently declares, in the most solemn and emphatic manner, the righteous and beneficent law of the survival of the fittest; a law which visits the iniquity of the fathers upon the children unto the third and fourth generation, and shows mercy unto thousands that love God and keep his commandments.

The Scotch-Irish Presbyterians, for generations, had been subjected to hardships, persecutions, and trials which had tended to secure in their descendants those physical and moral qualities that, pre-eminently, fitted them to be among the best of those hardy pioneers, who flung themselves, in successive waves of immigration, into the unexplored wildernesses of the North American continent. The striking qualities of this race were great powers of physical indurance, with corresponding energy and firmness of purpose; a clear and vigorous intellect; a faith as fixed as the rocks of that land from whence it came, and an all-pervading religious spirit, not always attractive or beautiful (how could it be, when the agent which had made it so strong, was bitter, unrelenting persecution?); but an all-pervading religious spirit, precisely what seemed to be required, to fit the race for the stern work that an All-Wise Providence, for many generations, had been preparing it. Looking back for several hundred years, we can see (I speak with all reverence) how the Most High seems to have prepared, through the formative influence of the law of natural selection, the earlier settlers of our country; the Puritans, the Huguenots, the Scotch-Irish Presbyterians, the Quakers, and the Roman Catholics under Lord Baltimore. Trial and persecutions were the sifting of Providence. None but the vigorous, none but the earnest, none but the strong of faith, none but the pure of purpose came in those early days. But these all were the chosen seed—the fit progenitors of the men who, one hundred years ago, founded our government.

Our friend, Dr. Hugh L. Hodge, came then of a vigorous and a godly race; his father, Hugh Hodge, a son of Andrew Hodge, preferring science to the commercial pursuits of his parent, studied medicine, and served as a surgeon in the Continental army during the War for Independence. After peace was declared, Dr. Hugh Hodge practised his profession in

Philadelphia; he married Maria Blanchard, of Boston, a descendant of the French Huguenots, a woman who afterwards proved herself worthy of her ancestral antecedents. In the dreadful epidemics of yellow fever in Philadelphia in 1793 and 1795, Dr. Hugh Hodge was distinguished for his heroism, and like so many other noble men in our profession, he fell a victim to his philanthropy, and died in 1798, leaving a widow and two sons; one of these sons is Professor Charles Hodge, of the Theological Seminary of Princeton; the other was our Professor, Dr. Hugh L. Hodge.

Medical men, as a class, are not rich, but the medical men of '93 and '95 were poor—their sublime self-devotion did not receive, neither did it seek, gold as its reward. Poverty is not, however, always an evil, and, if honorable, is usually the best inheritance a father can leave his sons. The doctor of the American Revolution, the martyr of the yellow fever epidemics, left his children but little of this world's goods, and yet he left them an inheritance more precious than untold thousands. Firm in faith, he left them to the mercies of that God he had served, and the histories of his two sons show how literally true the Mosaic declaration of the righteous law of natural selection is, how the best and noblest inheritance a young man can have, is an honorable descent from a race of good and true men.

I may be addressing some young men who are poor, some, perhaps, who have been compelled to practise the strictest self-denial to secure the means necessary to enable them to pursue their professional studies. To such, let me repeat the remark I have made, that honorable poverty is not an evil, but usually is a great blessing to every young man. When we study the lives of great men, we almost invariably find that, no matter how much they may have differed in other respects, yet they almost all began life poor; in other words, with them all, poverty was that essential school in which were acquired, or were strengthened, those qualities without which they could not have become great. To be a poor young man, then, means to be a young man to whom a kind Providence gives the noble opportunity of becoming great. Such was the school, such the moral and intellectual gymnasium that blessed the infancy and youth of our professor, and which, undoubtedly, were the means that made him what he was. His ancestral qualities, those of the Scotch-Irish Presbyterian and the Huguenot, hardened and strengthened by the wholesome discipline of poverty, moulded and directed by the tender care of a mother, whose only object in life was the education and moral development of her sons, and whose earliest teaching to these young athletes she was rearing, was the sublime answer to the first question of their dead father's confession of faith, that the "chief end of man is to glorify God."

At the age of fourteen, Hugh L. Hodge entered, as a Sophomore, Nassau Hall, Princeton, and graduated at the head of his class two years later. Beginning the study of medicine immediately, he became the private pupil of Dr. Caspar Wistar, and matriculated at the medical department of the University of Pennsylvania. He received the degree of Doctor of Medicine in 1818. Anxious to perfect himself in his profession, his great desire was to go to Europe, that he might continue his studies, but his means were not sufficient to accomplish his cherished wish. The young doctor, however, had too much firmness of will and fixedness of purpose to allow himself to be balked by such a trifle (to strong and earnest men) as poverty; he belonged to that favored class who possess the power of compelling fortune to do their bidding. Not having the money, he did not supinely wait, lamenting his hard lot that he was not among the favored ones of this earth, neither did he crave nor accept assistance from his rich friends, nor indulge in rash speculations, as is so much the custom in our day, in hope that some lucky "Flyer" might secure him the money he required. No, not having the money, he set about getting it in the good old-fashioned way of working for it, and honestly and slowly earning it. And this, let me remark, is the only sort of money that is worth possessing; it is that sort of money that sticks to a man, the kind that, like a domestic animal, comes into a man's house and becomes a willing member of his family. Money, acquired in any other way, is too apt to be like a wild and untamable animal, that cannot be domesticated; it is too apt to be that "riches that takes to itself wings and flies away."

Pursuing his manly purpose of conquering fortune, Dr. Hodge now sought and secured the position of surgeon on a vessel about to sail for India, hoping, by the ventures of the voyage, to realize enough money to enable him, on his return, to visit Europe, and there continue his professional studies. He sailed a few months after graduating, and returned safely in 1820. The voyage did not prove a commercial success, and our young doctor failed to bring back with him the means necessary to enable him to carry out his projected plan. His labor, however, was not lost; honest, manly, purposeful labor, even though it do not secure the object hoped for, is never lost. The law of the preservation and conversion of forces appears to be as absolute in morals as in physics. The young doctor came home light in pocket, but rich in a most varied and invaluable experience of men and things, an experience he never could have secured had he remained at home and hoped for success, instead of working hard to obtain it.

One of the most valuable of these experiences was that acquired by the study of the diseases of India, and more particularly by the study of Asiatic cholera, a disease at that time, viz. 1818, unknown both in Europe and America. Dr. Hodge saw and treated many cases of cholera, and thus obtained a knowledge of its symptoms and treatment which proved of inestimable value in the terrible cholera epidemic of 1832. During this fearful visitation, he was most active in the cholera hospitals, and was very successful in the plan of treatment he instituted. In commemoration of his faithful services, after the disappearance of the disease, the City presented him a silver pitcher and a vote of thanks.

On his return from India in 1820, Dr. Hodge, abandoning all hope of European study, began at once the practice of his profession in Philadelphia. He was elected about this time one of the physicians to the Southern Dispensary, and subsequently to the Philadelphia Dispensary. A year later, in 1821, he commenced his career as a teacher of medicine by taking charge of Dr. Horner's anatomical class while Dr. Horner visited Europe. This anatomical training most probably served to direct his attention more particularly to surgery, a branch for which he soon exhibited decided preference, and two years after, in 1823, he was elected a lecturer on the Principles of Surgery in the Association, which a few years later became the Medical Institute, lecturing in connection with Drs. Chapman, Dewees, Horner, Bell, Mitchell, Jackson, and T. Harris. About this time too he was appointed one of the Physicians to the Philadelphia Almshouse.

There are epochs in every man's history which determine his whole future; and the critical epochs in the life of Dr. Hodge were his marriage and his election as a Professor in the Medical Department of the University of Pennsylvania. The most solemn and important event in the life of every man who marries, is his marriage; the assumption of this sacred relation, with its grave and lifelong duties and responsibilities, is the one step on which will hang, in most cases, the whole future happiness of the individual. If this step be taken with wisdom and prudence, and with a due appreciation of all its weighty entailments, the results, other things being equal, almost necessarily will be the greatly increased happiness of the individual. If, however, the step be taken hastily, thoughtlessly, and in levity, the results almost necessarily will be the unhappiness, and often the destruction of both parties.

We could scarcely expect a man of the character and antecedents of our friend, to marry without serious consideration of all the solemn consequences of his act; he did not rashly and hastily, as so many young men do, marry before reaching the age of complete manhood, and before he had secured such a position in his profession as justified him in assuming not only the responsibilities and duties of married life, but also the greatly increased expenditures inevitable upon it. At the age of thirty-two years, after having been established in a rapidly increasing practice for several years, on November 12th, 1828, he married Margaret E. Aspinwall, a daughter of John Aspinwall, a well-known merchant of New York, and a granddaughter of Joseph Howland, of the same city, a descendant of John Howland, one of the May Flower pilgrims. The consequences of a step so wisely and prudently taken were most fortunate and happy. It would not be seemly here, however, to discuss the relations of domestic life ; seven sons were born of this union, five of whom survive their father. Mrs. Hodge died several years before her husband.

About the time of, and shortly after his marriage, certain circumstances happened which entirely changed the direction of his efforts, and the character of his practice. These circumstances were the failing health and advanced age of the two prominent obstetricians of Philadelphia, Dr. Thomas C. James, Professor of Obstetrics and of Diseases of Women and Children in the University of Pennsylvania, and Dr. Wm. P. Dewees. At the solicitation of these two gentlemen, he abandoned the specialty of surgery, to which he had for some years devoted himself, and began to apply himself to the practice and teaching of obstetrics. In consequence of this change in his plans of professional effort, when Dr. Dewees resigned the lectureship of Obstetrics in the Medical Institute, Dr. Hodge retired from his lectureship on Surgery, and was given that of Obstetrics; and, about the same time, and in furtherance of the same views, he was elected one of the Physicians to the Lying-in Department of the Pennsylvania Hospital.

As I have already remarked, the two great epochs in the life of our friend were his marriage, and his election to the Chair of Obstetrics and Diseases of Women and Children in the University of Pennsylvania. This latter event occurred in November, 1835, and it may not be uninteresting, here, to recall some circumstances in the history of the chair to which he was now elevated. In 1810, after a long and animated contest, in which Dr. Dewees and Dr. Nathaniel Chapman were his most active opponents, Dr. Thomas C. James was elected Professor of Obstetrics and of Diseases of Women and Children in the University of Pennsylvania. In 1834, Dr. James resigned his chair, and Dr. Wm. P. Dewees, who had assisted him for nine years, was appointed his successor. Dr. Dewees had aspired to this position for a quarter of a century, but was destined to hold it for a very short time—an apoplectic attack in 1834 greatly weakened his powers. In the autumn of 1835, he made an attempt to deliver his course of lectures, but found himself unable to continue, and he suddenly resigned his professorship on the 10th of November, 1835. The contest for the vacant chair was very close and exciting, it was decided, however, in favor of our friend, and Dr. Hugh L. Hodge was elected the professor.

At this crisis in his affairs, he was thirty-nine years of age—he had practised his profession for fifteen years, and had taught it for fourteen years; in other words, he was a fully matured man, thoroughly prepared, by study and experience, for the responsible and elevated position in which he had been placed, as well as peculiarly fitted for it by his antecedents and character. He entered now on a career of honor and usefulness, in which he was destined to continue for considerably over the third of a century. The classes of young men to which he lectured were very large, and were drawn from all parts of the United States, and soon his reputation as a teacher and as a practitioner became national. Patients came to him in great numbers from distant places, and these, when added to a very extensive home practice, kept him constantly occupied. Year by year this professional pressure increased, until at last he was obliged to relinquish, almost absolutely, his obstetrical practice, and to devote himself exclusively to the treatment of the diseases of females. In the management of these diseases his success was very great—his cardinal principle was, that the chief cause, not the sole cause, but the chief cause of the so-called diseases peculiar to women, was due to, I quote his own words, "a morbid irritation of the nerves of the parts, with or without congestion, but usually with no inflammation," that the cause of this morbid irritation, in most cases, was displacement of the uterus and its appendages, and that its rational treatment consisted in obviating the action of this cause by the use of mechanical supports, called pessaries.

Dr. Dewees, Dr. Hodge's predecessor, had done much good, both by his teachings and writings, in directing the attention of the medical profession to the influence of uterine displacements in causing female diseases. Dewees also had made great improvements in the form and material of these instruments, recommending glass and metal instead of the perishable substances then resorted to, as wood and cork. Indeed, the Dewees concavo-convex glass pessary is used even to this day, though now the glass is substituted by hard rubber, as a safer and better material.

A friend has furnished me with some very interesting facts in connection with the mechanical treatment of female disease by Dr. Hodge. The case, which first attracted his attention to the value of mechanical support, occurred in 1830, about the time he began to devote himself to obstetrics and the diseases of females. It was that of a woman, who had been admitted into the medical wards of the almshouse, supposed to be suffering from hepatic disease. This woman was subjected to the usual treatment for such affections, part of which treatment was a course of mercury; but in spite of everything done for her relief, she became rapidly worse. About this time, the resident physician who had charge of the patient, discovered, on making an examination, that there was decided retroversion of the uterus. He introduced one of the, then new, Dewees pessaries, and, to the astonishment of all, the liver complaint was cured, and the woman was speedily restored to health. The results of this case made a great impression on Dr. Hodge, and no doubt served to direct his attention more particularly to the teachings of Dewees, Gooch, and other writers of that day, who maintained the doctrine of distant sympathies long before the discoveries of Marshall Hall and later observers revealed to us the nature and cause of these sympathies. The lessons, taught by this instructive case of the almshouse patient, fell on good ground, and soon bore much fruit.

His opportunities, both public and private, for observing female diseases at this time, were becoming very great, and the results of these observations served only, year by year, to confirm him in the views he had begun to hold, as to the consequences of uterine displacements and their rational treatment.

When Dr. Hodge began, in 1830, the treatment of female

diseases as a specialty, the mechanical appliances in use were of the most limited character; there was no speculum, no uterine sound, no sponge-tent to aid in the diagnosis and treatment of these, in those days, necessarily, very obscure cases. Pessaries, though improved by Dewees, were still very imperfect in shape and arrangement. Dr. Hodge, for years, devoted himself to the discovery of the proper materials and shapes for these instruments. This investigation required not only great intelligence, but the utmost patience and the most unwearied perseverance. Year by year he groped, as it were, in search of these unknown quantities, viz., the size, the shapes, and the material of uterine supports; at last he found them, not all at once or all together, but far apart and at long intervals, and only after a persistent search, the difficulties of which would have balked most men at the outset. He sometimes, to illustrate the character of this search and the nature of these difficulties, exhibited to his friends a number of large drawers containing hundreds, perhaps, thousands, of contrivances of every possible shape and material, which he called his "collection of abortions;" and these were the implements he had used in his gropings after the sought-for unknown quantities.

Dr. Hodge once told a friend how the idea of the lever pessary first came to him. He had been contemplating for a long time the subject of new shapes for pessaries, and, after many experiments, had found nothing satisfactory. One evening, while sitting alone in the room where the meetings of the medical faculty of the University were held, his eyes rested on the upright steel support by the fireplace, designed to hold the shovel and tongs; the shovel and tongs were kept in position by a steel hook, and, as he surveyed the supporting curve of this hook, the longed-for illumination came; the shape, apparently so paradoxical, revealed itself in the glowing light and flickering flame of the burning grate, and the Hodge lever pessary was the result. No discovery has ever been made in the treatment of female diseases which has done more good than this original conception of Dr. Hodge. The lever pessary is now universally recognized, abroad as well as in this country, as *the* instrument for the treatment, of most forms, of uterine displacement. Like the forceps of Chamberlen, it has received innumerable modifications, none of which, however, are improvements, and the simple open and closed lever pessaries of Hodge must always remain the perfect types of the lever pessary.

Dr. Hodge used at first, as the material for the new pessaries, very thin silver plated with gold, but, after the discovery of hard rubber, this material was found so perfectly adapted to the construction of such instruments that, save in exceptional cases, it is now the only one used. At first the only lever pessary employed was the open lever, but, gradually, he perfected his discovery by giving the instrument its double curve and making it closed, and it is in this latter form that it is now generally used.

The lever pessary, though an inestimable boon to suffering woman, is by no means the only gift of Dr. Hodge to his profession and to humanity. The Hodge eclectic forceps is a most valuable instrument; this instrument does not profess to be an original conception as the lever pessary is, but is rather the result of a sagacious eclecticism, taught by long experience and thorough knowledge of the force and mechanism of parturition. The eclectic forceps is so well known, it is unnecessary I should say of it more than that, in the great number of modifications which the obstetrical forceps has received, none are better and few as good as the Hodge modification.

Dr. Hodge made many other contributions to the surgery of his specialty; among them, I may mention his instruments for embryotomy comprising his modification of Baudelocque's cephalotribe, named by him "compressores cranii," and his craniotomy scissors; also, a modified forceps for extracting retained placenta after abortion, as well as a lever and crochet, in one piece, for use in abortion, and in removing certain forms of pessaries.

No man of his generation, except, perhaps, the late Prof. Simpson, of Edinburgh, did so much for his special department of practice as our Professor; and, while we accord to the Edinburgh Professor all the honor due his great originality and his untiring efforts in the advancement of science, we still turn lovingly and admiringly to our dear friend, Dr. Hugh L. Hodge, and say he had not his peer.

As a teacher of medicine, Dr. Hodge was most widely and favorably known. His style was characterized by great purity, dignity, and earnestness. His intellect was too strong, and his experience too great to permit him to follow, blindly, the theories and teachings of others, and hence his lectures were markedly original, and he never hesitated boldly to differ from doctrines, though almost universally accepted, when he believed them false. His relations with his classes were of the most pleasant character ; the students loved and revered him, and the old Alumni of the University will re- call, with tender recollections, the benign and intellectual countenance, the deep and manly tones of their beloved Pro- fessor, as he earnestly endeavored to impress upon them some point which he deemed of great importance.

His teachings were of the most reliable kind, no crude theories or hastily formed opinions were given to the young men who received their knowledge from his lips. Every one who listened to him felt, from the first sentence they heard, how completely their Professor realized the great responsibility of his position, and how every opinion ex- pressed and direction given had been most carefully, and conscientiously reached, after years of study and experi- ence. His great desire seemed to be to instruct his class, not in what was most new, but in those things which his obser- vation told him were true ; hence, the memories of his stu- dents were not crowded with ephemeral theories, supported by imaginary facts, but were stored with truth, which, like pure gold, is always treasure, and never becomes old-fash- ioned.

It is now more than a quarter of a century since I, as a medical student, first had the great advantage of being taught by him. Since then, I have had much to unlearn, but I never had to unlearn what he taught me as true, and to this day, I profess myself, a believer in and an advocate of the views taught by Dr. Hodge twenty-five years ago.

Dr. Hodge possessed an excellent constitution, his health was always extraordinarily good, and I have often heard him

2

say, that he had not taken a dose of medicine for years, and that the only remedy he ever required or took was plenty of hot water. His uninterrupted good health, undoubtedly, was due to his naturally good constitution, as well as to his mode of life, which was strictly in keeping with the character of a man whose eating, drinking, and doing were always done, not for self-gratification, but with a conscientious regard to the duties and obligations of life. Hence, his personal habits were frugal, and he allowed himself none of those indulgences which most men, especially when engaged in laborious and exacting pursuits, look upon as their right. He was sparing in the use of wine, and totally opposed to tobacco, against which he always expressed a most relentless and vigorous antagonism.

But years of constant labor, grave anxieties, and weighty responsibilities will, at last, tell on the most perfect constitution, and they found their expression in Dr. Hodge through his eyesight. His eyes had been severely taxed by his studious habits as a youth and as a younger man, and now gradually began to fail—the trouble appeared to be a weakness in the optic nerve, and one, therefore, which could not be relieved by surgical skill. With advancing years came increasing feebleness of vision, until at last he was unable to use his eyes for reading or writing, and was compelled to employ an amanuensis to conduct even his business correspondence. This infirmity finally determined him to relinquish his professorial duties, and in April, 1863, he resigned his chair—a position which he had filled for twenty-eight years, with so much credit to himself and so much honor and advantage to this school. The Board of Trustees, on accepting his resignation, elected him the Emeritus Professor.

When Dr. Hodge resigned his professorship, he generously presented to the Trustees of the University his very valuable museum, together with the whole of his collection of material used by him in illustrating his lectures, obtained at great cost, and the accumulations of the twenty-eight years of his incumbency. In making this gift, he coupled it with the request that the collection should be kept distinct from the general museum of the school, and that it should always be under the curatorship of the Professor of Obstetrics.

During the earlier years of his professional life, Dr. Hodge was so completely engrossed with the cares of practice and teaching, that he had no time to contribute much to the literature of his profession. As a young man, he was one of the editors of the "North American Medical and Surgical Journal," which journal was organized and conducted by the members of the Kappa Lambda Association. His associate editors in this undertaking were Drs. Franklin Bache, Charles D. Meigs, B. H. Coates, and René La Roche, of which distinguished corps, Dr. Coates is now the sole survivor. To this and other journals he contributed, at times, reviews and original articles, among which was a valuable article on Aneurism, which was contributed to the "American Cyclopædia of Practical Medicine and Surgery."

In 1860, he published his work on Diseases Peculiar to Women, including Displacements of the Uterus. The object of the author, and I use as nearly as possible his own language, "was to present more at length and in detail those views on the nervous diseases of women, which he had for so many years taught in the halls of the University." He wished to inculcate " not merely what he deemed a more correct theory and practice in inflammatory disease of the uterus, but to insist that a very large proportion of the so-called cases of metritis are, in reality, but examples of irritation, where inflammation has subsided, or where it actually never existed," indeed, the chief object of the whole work is to exemplify the nature, consequences, and treatment of nervous irritation as distinct from inflammation. Convinced by long experience, the author shows (I still use his own language) that the uterus is involved in most of these complaints, and that its disturbances are very frequently dependent upon displacements of the organ, and hence, the book is largely devoted to the subject of displacements of the uterus, and their mechanical treatment.

Dr. Hodge's opportunities for observing and treating female diseases were unusually great. Large numbers of patients came to Philadelphia to consult him, and these, it must be remembered, were not ordinary cases of sickness, but in most instances were cases which had been under medical treatment for long periods without benefit. His success in managing these, heretofore, incurable cases, was often very striking, and hundreds of women who came to Philadelphia helpless and hopeless invalids, returned to their homes restored, by our Professor's skill, to health, usefulness, and happiness. After thirty years of this sort of experience, he produced this book—the result of a lifetime of observation, and he tells us in it how he brought about these wonderful recoveries.

The work was not quickly or hastily composed; its material had been thoroughly digested; for thirty years the fire had burned, and when he spoke, it was with a force and originality characteristic of the man. His sight at this time was so imperfect that all of his reading was done by the eyes of another, and this, no doubt, accounts for the almost entire absence in the volume of everything not original with himself. In the introduction he gives the opinions of others; in the book itself he gives his own opinions, and every word and every sentence of it show careful thought.

On resigning the duties of his professorship, Dr. Hodge devoted himself to the completion of a work he had contemplated for years. In this work he proposed giving (I again use his own words) "the results of his experience and reflection on the theory and practice of Obstetrics, fulfilling, by so doing, an imperative duty he owed to the Alumni and Trustees of the University, by presenting in an extended form, the peculiar doctrines and practice inculcated by him while Professor of Obstetrics;" and he deemed this duty, he tells us, "the more binding, because thirty-eight years had elapsed since the first edition of Dr. Dewees's Midwifery."

This great work on Obstetrics was completed in a year after relinquishing his professorship, and was published in 1864; it was dedicated to the memory of Thomas C. James and Wm. P. Dewees, the first and second Professors of Obstetrics in the University of Pennsylvania. In the preface to this book the writer assures us that, "he does not inculcate the opinions merely of others; that, though the reading of authors has been of use to him, nature has been of much more;" he gives, therefore, he tells us, without reserve, "his own opinion on all points;" and "consequently, he is often in opposition to the most admired authors."

Dr. Hodge had devoted himself, for a long time, to the careful study of the mechanism of labor ; and, in his book, a considerable space is occupied by this important subject, in the discussion of which he displays great originality, both in the singularly excellent illustrations which he has devised, as well as in the new and valuable conclusions which he has reached.

This "System of Obstetrics," whether we estimate it by the learning, research, and care which its pages display, or by its original teachings and illustrations, or by the philosophical character as well as great force and clearness of its instruction, must be ranked among the very first works on Obstetrics ever issued from the American or foreign press. Dr. Hodge, in this book, gives us his teachings as Professor of Obstetrics in the University of Pennsylvania for twenty-eight years ; and the thousands of the Alumni of the University, who, during this long period, had the good fortune to be instructed by him, as well as those who have graduated since, will always turn with pride, pleasure, and profit, to this noble work of their old Professor.

After resigning his professorship, in addition to the preparation and supervision of his books, Dr. Hodge contributed valuable papers on obstetrical subjects to the medical journals; and, at the same time, was engaged in a very extensive practice in the treatment of diseases of females. In 1872 the title of LL.D. was conferred upon him by Nassau Hall, Princeton.

A recent and highly esteemed writer on psychology says: "the history of a man is the true revelation of his character ; what he has done indicates what he has willed ; what he has willed marks what he has thought and felt, or the character of his deliberations; what he has thought and felt has been the result of his nature, then existing, as the developmental products of a certain original constitution, and a definite life experience." In the history of our friend, which I am now giving you, I have endeavored to trace out the elements, both inherited and accidental, which contributed to form his character. I have tried to show that great men and great deeds are not the results of accident, but are the direct and necessary consequence of certain and numerous antecedent conditions.

That I might be able to exhibit our friend's character in its truest and, therefore, in its best light, so that none of its instructive and noble lessons might be lost, I requested Dr. Caspar Morris, who was his lifelong and most intimate friend, as well as his family physician, and who, if ever man knew his fellow, knew Dr. Hodge, to furnish me with a sketch of his character. This he did, in a letter to me, which is so admirable that I feel I should be doing injustice both to Dr. Morris and to my subject were I not to give it almost verbatim. With Dr. Morris's consent, therefore, omitting mainly a few lines referring to points already discussed, I introduce here his letter as I received it.

"It was through the intervention of Dr. James and Dr. Dewees that I was thrown into the intimate relations with Dr. Hodge, which, thanks to his unvarying character, continued to become more and more close and unreserved to the day of his death. Few outside the sacred precincts of the nearest domestic relations, have ever enjoyed an equally favorable opportunity for knowing the true character of another, and in the clear light of this near approach, I do not hesitate to describe him as more justly entitled to the character of a 'perfect man' than any man I have ever known. Apparently incongruous elements were in him harmoniously blended; perfect integrity in his own dealings was united with the most lenient view of the deviations of others; and unflinching courage in his own adherence to what he believed to be right, with the most delicate recognition of difficulties which turned aside from the path of duty those who did not possess the same inflexible principle. In describing his character, I know no better course than the presentation of the germ from which the whole was developed; the corner-stone on which the edifice reposed. Regarding him in his relations

as a man to his fellow men, a citizen to his fellow country-
men, as a physician to his patients, in all these varied relations
of life, he acted under the sense of strict integrity and duty.
If it were proper to penetrate into the more sacred precincts
of domestic life, we should there find the same influence controlling the most delicate relations of husband and father.
Beyond this no one dare intrude, yet the rays of a still deeper
life burst through the veil by which the holy of holies was
screened from outward observation, and proved that in it was
the fountain of light which gave energy to the whole; hence
arose the entire harmony of his character. No man was
ever more justly entitled to the honor of the description of
the perfect man, given by the poet nearly twenty centuries
ago, the gem-like purity of which never suffers from the fre-
quency of handling, nor allows it to become trite by repeti-
tion. He was ' Propositi tenacem,' well rendered by

> ' He holds no parley with unmanly fears,
> Where duty calls incontinently steers.'

Yet this fixedness of purpose and perseverance in action,
which when dissociated from careful circumspection, sound
judgment, and high principle degenerates into mere obstinacy,
rarely betrayed Dr. Hodge into error. It was his highest
merit that he never failed to examine carefully, laboriously,
and diligently whatever subject claimed his consideration;
and it was not until he had viewed it in all its relations, and
examined its bearings with the utmost scrutiny that he adopted his opinion. This once done, that opinion became to him,
on that point, the symbol of truth, and as such was built into
its appropriate place in the structure of his mind—became an
integral part of himself. There were no subsequent ques-
tionings on that point; he never incurred the risk of over-
turning the entire superstructure by removing, or taking out
to dress over again, a stone already placed; he would rather
doubt the truth of a new observation than that of one already
thoroughly examined, carefully tested, and accurately ad-
justed; and he never laid any one in its position until it
had been thus prepared. The success he achieved in his
various undertakings was mainly owing to this peculiarity

of his character. If a difficulty presented itself, it was not as an obstacle to arrest, but as an opposition to be overcome. He never knew what it was to be defeated, nor though his feelings were as sensitive, and his sympathies as acute as those of a woman, did he ever shrink or quail before any suffering which was to be encountered by himself or his patient in the conflict with disease.

"As a teacher he had rendered himself perfectly familiar with all the elemental forms, as well as the more complicated connections, of professional knowledge; and, having made them his own, he brought them to bear, for the benefit of his patients, under circumstances where the conviction of the soundness and perfection of his knowledge gave him support. It was not only in the emergencies of unnatural labor, but, in the equally trying difficulties of the gynæcologist, that he found the benefit of this support, which enabled him to persevere, in ever-renewed efforts, until he achieved results which fully rewarded his labors, as well as justified the soundness of his principles.

"No better illustration of his character can be presented than that afforded by the history of his treatment of cases of chronic uterine disease. Confident that congestions, inflammations, and so-called ulcerations were more generally, if not always, the results of displacements of the uterus, he early set himself to the discovery of some apparatus to support that organ, and one had but to look at the vast collection of instruments of various material and infinite variety of form, which accumulated in his drawers, to recognize how earnestly and patiently he strove to accomplish his object. Who ever knew Dr. Hodge to abandon a case as hopeless? Who ever knew him to hesitate to make new efforts for relief or cure when disappointed by failure? If one form of pessary was found inappropriate, another was to be tried, and if one instrument was not sufficient, a second, or even a third, would be added to afford the support needed. Day after day he would return, and hour after hour he would spend at the bedside in unwearying efforts to secure the desired adjustment. Hundreds of patients were promptly relieved from chronic ailments and prolonged suffering by his well-adapted treatment, and many a wretched invalid blesses his memory for the unwearied patience which he gave to that mechanical adjustment, which, when at last secured, brought her health and happiness. The picture would not be complete, however, did it not represent the gentle forbearance with which he met discontented complaints and irritating fretfulness sometimes displayed by patients and friends unable to comprehend the difficulties to be encountered. No one ever witnessed the failure of that forbearance or heard from Dr. Hodge one expression of discontent, even when most unjustly censured. 'As patient as Hodge,' became, among his professional friends, the expression of a degree of possession of that great virtue which was not to be surpassed.

"To Dr. Hodge's well-founded convictions that he designed to do what was right, and, before acting, always endeavored to ascertain what was proper to be done, may be referred his absolute freedom from petty squabbles with his patients, or more serious strife with professional friends or rivals, which was a marked peculiarity of his character. While holding his own views on the doctrines of medical science and the ethics of professional relations, as positively as man can hold opinions, he never failed to recognize the rights of others to be equally positive in holding and acting on their own convictions. In looking back on my long intimacy with Dr. Hodge I can recall no instance of personal quarrel with either professional rival or competitor. This did not arise from any weakness on his part, or failure to express his dissent from what he regarded as erroneous opinions. The dearest friendship never led him to withhold the clearest and simplest expression of his own opinions, widely divergent as they might be, from those of his colleagues or friends, and no one could feel hurt by the clear expression of views so honestly and firmly held. He esteemed truth sacred in all its applications, and neither fear nor hope of favor could influence him to any deviation in his conduct from its clear dictates. An ever-present influence, stimulating to constant effort, was his desire to do what he believed to be right. The following incident will exhibit the extent of its power:—

"Among his college friends were some who attained great

eminence as ministers of the gospel, and with whom he ever maintained the intimacy of early association. On one occa sion, when several of these friends were sitting with him, in the abandon of friendship, the subject of the use of tobacco and its effects on the nervous system was brought up; the discussion took a jovial turn—one of the reverend gentlemen present defended its use, and declared his contempt for those who made apologies for it on the score of its medical proper- ties; he said 'he used tobacco, not because it was good for him, but because he liked it.' Dr. Hodge expressed his opinion that tobacco was decidedly depressing to the nerve force, as well as exhausting to the vital energy, and thus its use became an incentive to a resort to alcoholic beverages; and, rising from his seat in the midst of the discussion, he advanced to his friend, laying his hands on his shoulders and looking him solemnly in the face, said, 'I adjure you, in the name of the Saviour you love, to lay aside this indulgence.' The right reverend gentleman, to whom this admonition was addressed, has told me that, at the moment, he felt much hurt by Dr. Hodge's manner, but that the appeal was so solemn and so powerful, he could not get rid of its impression, and he never was able to use tobacco afterwards; and this, he said, was the harder, because he had just received a valuable pre- sent of a large supply of excellent quality. This same earnest- ness and decision marked his relations in domestic life, and gave tone and power to his religious character.

"His faith in the simple fundamental principles of the Christ- ian religion was as firmly fixed as his conviction of the truth of a demonstrated problem in mathematics. He was not in the habit of talking much on the subject, and never about his own feelings or experience. There was nothing obtrusive in his religion; like the light which gives beauty to the foliage, color to the flower, and nutriment to the fruit, it inspired and gave beauty and strength to all his actions, and needed no blowing of trumpets to announce itself. He was a devout attendant on the means of grace, whenever the duties of his profession did not oppose insuperable obstacles, and was pro- fusely liberal in his pecuniary contributions to the support of the ministry of the gospel, while in quiet unostentatious alms-giving he was most munificent. The claims on Dr. Hodge's charity were great and unceasing, and many a sufferer, poor in this world's goods, who sought relief from his professional skill, found that, instead of thinking he had performed his part in giving his time and labor, he willingly embraced the opportunity, afforded by the intimacy of professional relations, to contribute to their pecuniary necessities, and these contributions, in some instances, he always afterwards kept up.

" Dr. Hodge was a very laborious student, and notwithstanding the loss of his sight, which obliged him to resort to the assistance of an amanuensis and a reader, he continued to the last to devote many hours daily to the revision of his works, and the careful study of those topics which were embraced in them. Few would suspect that his great work on obstetrics was produced under circumstances so disadvantageous. We have been accustomed to think of Milton's blindness as adding to the value of his immortal poem, and that of Prescott, as a serious obstacle to the acquisition of the knowledge displayed in his histories, which have added lustre to American literature, but neither of these encountered difficulties so great as those overcome by Dr. Hodge in the production of his works, marked, as they are, by such minute accuracy in detail, in forms, shapes, and measurements, and illustrated as they are by photographs of subjects and specimens he could not see, and for his acquaintance with which he was dependent on the eyes and descriptions of others. His will, indeed, was indomitable, and led him never to admit any apology for abandoning, neglecting, or escaping from the performance of any duty on account of the difficulties involved in doing it.

" He delighted in the exertion of his powers, and might daily be seen groping his way from his carriage to the doors and chambers of his patients, refusing the proffered arm of those who saw his almost absolute blindness. Within twelve hours of the attack which so abruptly terminated his labors I had earnestly remonstrated with him against his exposing himself on one of the coldest days of a winter of noted severity, only, however, to elicit from him, in playful response, a reproach of my own indulgence in yielding to the influence he so successfully resisted. No one who knew the man, and who could estimate the value of the principles by which he was actuated in everything he did, could do otherwise than reverence the inflexible perseverance in doing his duty to God and man, which marked his entire life; obstinacy, if it had arisen from any meaner motive, it became sublime self-devotion in his beautiful character."

After this admirable picture of his friend's character, which Dr. Morris has furnished, there is left but little for me to add.

When Dr. Hodge resigned his professorship, he was in the sixty-seventh year of his age; he had reached and passed the period when most men cease to work, and yet, save his infirmity of vision, his faculties were perfect. His form was erect, his step elastic, his hearing acute, while his intellect was as clear and his sympathies as quick as ever. It was my good fortune to meet him in consultation a few weeks before his death; as we went from the parlor to the bed-chamber of our patient he ran lightly up the stairs. I remarked upon his agility, when he playfully replied, "Oh! I am too young to walk up stairs."

He took great interest in all the religious and philanthropic movements of the day, and was active in the affairs of the church, of which he was a member, and was most generous in his benefactions to it, and to other good causes. He gave, however, something of incomparably greater value than money. He enriched the medical profession, and did good to the world, not only by the books which he wrote, and the instruments he devised, but, by a life and an example that will not soon lose their influence. This great doctor—this learned professor—this munificent giver—this man who was looked up to by the community in which he lived, and by the profession which he adorned, was, at the same time, the devout and humble believer, with the spirit and the faith of a little child; and though his praise was in all the churches, yet he esteemed himself among the least of the brethren. It might be imagined, perhaps, that such a man was a stern man—one who viewed with disfavor everything that was bright and cheerful; but, the very reverse was the case; an earnest religious spirit, indeed, was the pervading principle of his life—a spirit entirely incompatible with levity or frivolity, and yet, a spirit which made him uniformly cheerful, serene, and happy. No one approached him who did not see and feel this in his genial and gracious smile, or hear it in his tender and sympathetic, or in his kind and gentle tones. To him life implied work, progress, constant improvement, and he held, as has been well expressed, that "to the brave man this world is full to the brim of happiness, and that the future is as certain as the truthfulness of God." Thus he lived.

Thus he died. The day preceding his last illness he appeared to be in his usual excellent health, and he was occupied, until late in the afternoon, with his professional engagements. On this very day, too, he spent some hours preparing an article on Cephalotripsy, at which he had been working for several weeks. He retired to rest at his usual bedtime, seeming perfectly well, and in good spirits. Near midnight he was seized with nausea, faintness, failure of the heart's action, and of respiration, and died twenty-six hours after—sustained, to the last, by that faith he had learned at his mother's knee, that strong faith he had inherited from a pious race, which, generations before, had sacrificed country and home for religious freedom.

The setting sun, as he sinks, into apparent oblivion, behind that jealous horizon which receives him after his work is done, illuminates, with an indescribable splendor, the very mists and clouds that help to obscure him, and as his light at last goes out, celestial bodies appear in the heavens, looking down, as it were, upon the field of their departed brother's work and usefulness. The splendor of the sunset is of the earth, and only tells of a passing day; but the celestial forms that come after, speak of the Infinite and the Eternal. Our friend, as he sank into apparent oblivion behind that jealous horizon, which bounds our mortal vision, illumined its dark cloud with a truly heavenly glory, and though they, who lovingly waited and watched, until the light faded and the darkness came, though they did *not* see celestial forms, yet we may feel sure that, if ever, human soul was met by rejoicing throngs as it entered the portals of the blessed, *his was so met.*

The following is a list of the chief articles and books published by Dr. Hodge :—

Observations on Expansibility as a Vital Property, and on the Influence of the Capillary Tissue over the Circulation of the Blood. By Hugh L. Hodge, M.D., Lecturer on the Principles of Surgery in the Medical Institute. North American Medical and Surgical Journal, vol. 6, No. xi. 1828.

The Article on Aneurism, in the American Cyclopædia of Practical Medicine and Surgery.

Cases of Peritonitis, with Remarks. By Hugh L. Hodge, M.D., one of the Physicians to the Almshouse. North American Med. and Surg. Journ., vol 7, No. xiv. 1829.

Cases and Observations regarding Puerperal Fever, as it prevailed in the Pennsylvania Hospital, in February and March, 1833. By Hugh L. Hodge, M.D., one of the Physicians of that Charity. Amer. Journ. Med. Sciences, August, 1833.

On the Pathology and Therapeutics of Cholera Maligna. By Hugh L. Hodge, one of the Physicians of the Almshouse Infirmary, and late Physician to the City Cholera Hospital, No. 4. Amer. Journ. Med. Sciences, August, 1833.

Introductory and Valedictory Addresses. Published 1835, 36, 38, 39, 40, 47, 50, 52, 59.

Memoir of Thomas C. James, M.D., read before the College of Physicians of Philadelphia. By Hugh L. Hodge, M.D., Professor of Obstetrics, etc. etc., in the University of Pennsylvania, June, 1841.

An Eulogium on William P. Dewees, M.D., delivered before the medical students of the University of Pennsylvania, November 5, 1842. By Hugh L. Hodge, M.D., Professor of Obstetrics, etc. etc.

Diseases Peculiar to Women, including Displacements of the Uterus. By Hugh L. Hodge, M.D., Professor of Obstetrics and Diseases of Women and Children in the University of Pennsylvania. Philadelphia ; Blanchard & Lea. 1860.

The Principles and Practice of Obstetrics. Illustrated with one hundred and fifty-nine lithographic figures, from original photographs, and with numerous wood-cuts. By Hugh L. Hodge, M.D., Emeritus Professor of Obstetrics and Diseases of Women and Children in the University of Pennsylvania, lately one of the Physicians to the Lying-in Department of the Pennsylvania Hospital, lately one of the Physicians to the Philadelphia Almshouse Hospital, Consulting Physician to the Philadelphia Dispensary, Fellow of the College of Physicians of Philadelphia, Member of the American Philosophical Society, etc. etc. Author of a Treatise on "The Peculiar Diseases of Women." Philadelphia : Blanchard & Lea. 1864.

"Fœticide" (being a reprint, with some additions, of Introductory Lecture on Criminal Abortion). By Hugh L. Hodge, M.D. Philadelphia: Lindsay & Blakiston. 1869.

On the "Synclitism of the Fœtal Head in Natural Labor." By Hugh L. Hodge, M.D., Emeritus Professor of Obstetrics and Diseases of Women and Children in the University of Pennsylvania. Amer. Journ. Med. Sciences, October, 1870.

On the "Synclitism of the Equatorial Plane of the Fœtal Head in Pelvic Deliveries." By Hugh L. Hodge, M.D., Emeritus Professor, etc. etc. Amer. Journ. Med. Sciences, July, 1871.

www.ingramcontent.com/pod-product-compliance
Lightning Source LLC
Chambersburg PA
CBHW021453090426
42739CB00009B/1737